Snake

me

Bee

Inky

Name: ....

Class: ....

School: ....

sh

Action
Place your finger over your lips and say *sh, sh, sh.*

am
get
clap
shop
fish
shut
wish
I
the
shampoo

Write an ‹sh› word in each fish and draw a picture to illustrate it.

Dictation

1. _____

2. _____

3. _____

4. _____

5. _____

6. _____

7. _____

8. _____

9. _____

ch

Action
Move your arms as if you are a train and say *ch, ch, ch*.

if

hot

blot

chips

lunch

chest

much

he

she

chicken

Write a ‹ch› word in each chest and draw a picture to illustrate it.

chest

Dictation

1.

2.

3.

4.

5.

6.

7.

8.

9.

4

Sentences

Put the words in the right order to make a sentence about the picture.

pond.	A	swims	duck	the	on

A

Put the words in the right order and color the picture.

to	The	run	chicks	nest.	the

Action

Stick out your tongue, a little for *th* and further for *th*.

us

sad

flag

this

with

that

thank

me

we

thinking

Write a ‹th› word in each thought bubble and draw a picture.

Dictation

1.

2.

3.

4.

5.

6.

7.

8.

9.

6

Are these sentences correct? Write out each sentence correctly on the line.

1. the dog is spotty.

2. The duck swims on the.

3. I sleep in a bunk bed.

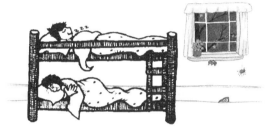

4. i like. eggs

5. They are playing ball.

ng

Action
Pretend to lift a heavy weight above your head and say *ng*.

in
leg
glad
ring
sang
strong
lung
be
was
length

Write an ‹ng› word in each ring and draw a picture to illustrate it.

ang

strength

ing

ong

ung

Dictation

1.

2.

3.

4.

5.

6.

7.

8.

9.

Capital Letters

Write the capital letter next to each lower-case letter.

A a   b   c   d   e

f   g   h   i   j

k   l   m   n   o

p   q   r   s   t

u   v   w   x   y   z

Join each capital letter to the matching lower-case letter.

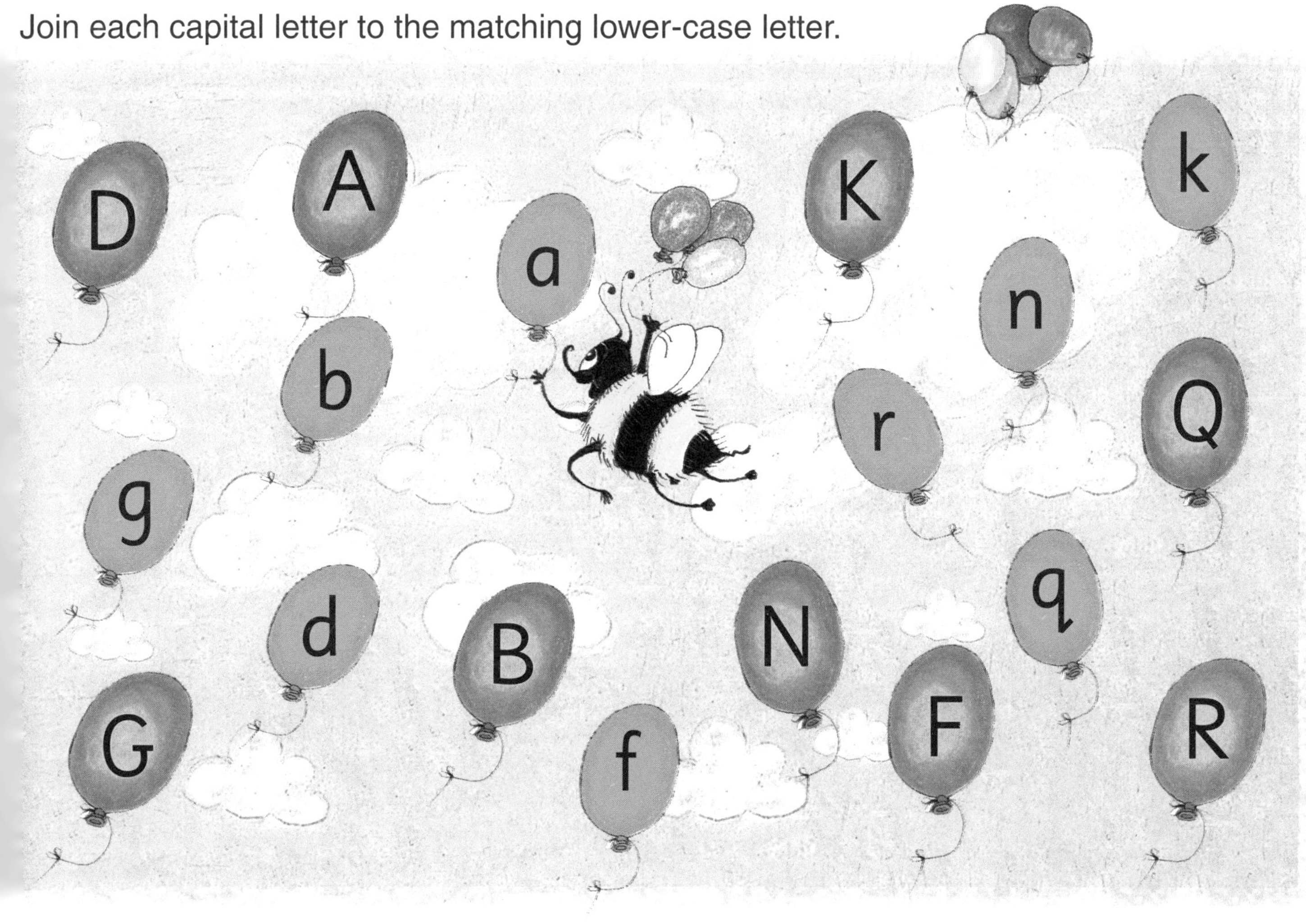

9

qu

Action
Make a duck's beak with your hands and say *qu, qu, qu*.

on
but
plum
quick
quiz
queen
squid
to
do
squirrel

Write a ‹qu› word in each duck and draw a picture to illustrate it.

Dictation

1.

2.

3.

4.

5.

6.

7.

8.

9.

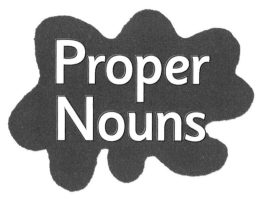 # Proper Nouns

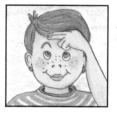

Action
Touch your forehead with your index and middle fingers.

Draw pictures of yourself and your teacher in the frames and write your names on the lines.

Me

My Teacher

_____

_____

Write your school's address on the envelope.

Action

Flap your hands like a seal's flippers and say *ar, ar, ar*.

at
yes
slug
arm
hard
scarf
card
are
all
farmyard

Write an ‹ar› word in each star and draw a picture to illustrate it.

Dictation

1.

2.

3.

4.

5.

6.

7.

8.

9.

12

Common Nouns

Action
Put your hand on your forehead.

Draw three pictures and write the nouns underneath.

_____   _____   _____

Write a noun in the gap and draw its picture in the box.

1. The _____ is black.

2. I throw the _____ .

3. A _____ can swim.

4. I like to eat _____ .

13

Fill each container with short vowel words. Write /a/ words in the bag, /e/ words in the net, /i/ words in the bin, /o/ words in the box, and /u/ words in the mug.

Vowel Hand

dog
bran
Monday
Tuesday
Wednesday
Thursday
Friday
you
your
Saturday

a bag

e net

i bin

o box

u mug

Dictation

1.

2.

3.

4.

5.

6.

7.

8.

9.

Alphabetical Order

Write the capital letters next to the lower-case letters.

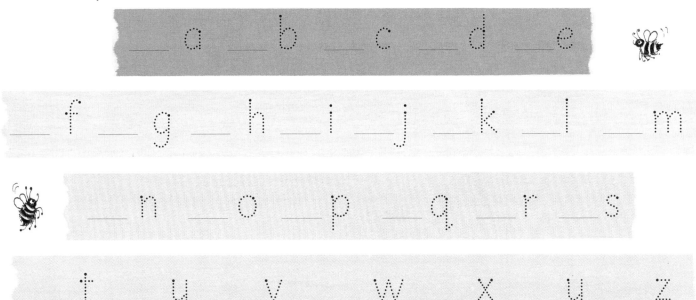

__ a __ b __ c __ d __ e

__ f __ g __ h __ i __ j __ k __ l __ m

__ n __ o __ p __ q __ r __ s

__ t __ u __ v __ w __ x __ y __ z

Which letters come before and after?

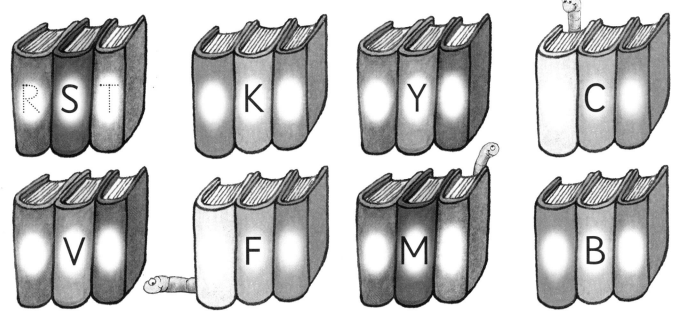

R S T | K | Y | C

V | F | M | B

Put these sets of letters into alphabetical order.

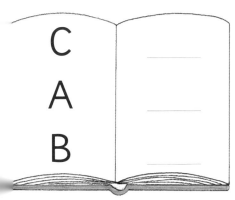

C A B

M L K

U V T

15

ff

up
man
crab
off
cliff
stiff
cuff
come
some
stuffing

Write an ‹ff› word in each cliff and draw a picture to illustrate it.

cliff

Dictation

1.

2.

3.

4.

5.

6.

7.

8.

9.

Write '**an**' before each word beginning with a vowel and write '**a**' before each word beginning with a consonant.

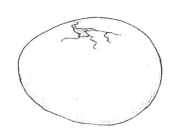

Aa Ee Ii Oo Uu

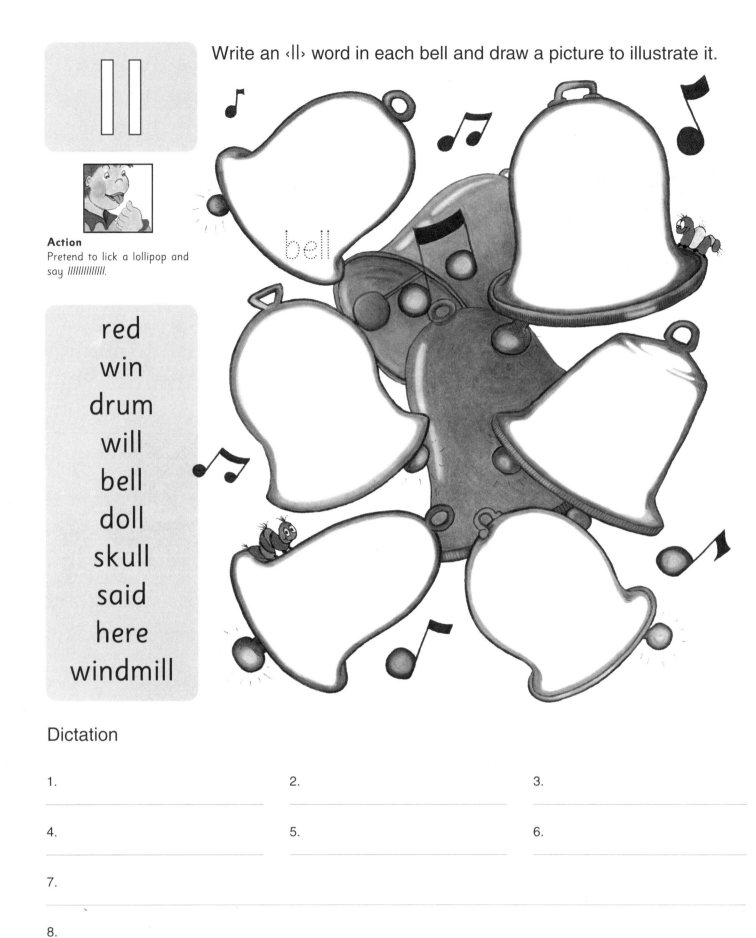

Write an ‹ll› word in each bell and draw a picture to illustrate it.

Action
Pretend to lick a lollipop and say *lllllllllll*.

red
win
drum
will
bell
doll
skull
said
here
windmill

bell

Dictation

1. _____

2. _____

3. _____

4. _____

5. _____

6. _____

7. _____

8. _____

9. _____

Plurals

Illustrate each word in the boxes.

hats	pens	dog
cars	cow	frog

Write the word for each picture.

_____

_____

Write an ‹ss› word in each dress and a ‹zz› word in the bee. Draw a picture for each word.

Action
Weave your hand in an ‹s› shape, saying *sssss*.

Action
Put your arms out like a bee's wings, and say *zzzzz*.

ox
run
from
buzz
cross
less
miss
there
they
crossroads

Dictation

1. _____

2. _____

3. _____

4. _____

5. _____

6. _____

7. _____

8. _____

9. _____

Pronouns

Draw a picture for each pronoun.
Remember to draw more than one person for the plural pronouns.

Singular Pronouns

I

Point to yourself.

you

Point to someone else.

he

Point to a boy.

she

Point to a girl.

it

Point to the floor.

we

Point in a circle to include yourself and others.

you

Point to two other people.

they

Point to the next-door class.

I   you

he   she   it

Plural Pronouns

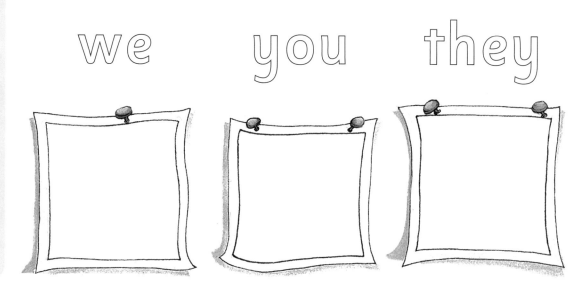

we   you   they

ck

Action
Snap your fingers together,
saying *ck, ck, ck.*

hop
fit
grin
duck
neck
clock
lick
go
no
broomstick

Write a ‹ck› word in each chick and draw a picture to illustrate it.

chick

Dictation

1.

2.

3.

4.

5.

6.

7.

8.

9.

22

Initial Consonant Blends

Read the initial consonant blends around the edge of the page and trace inside them.
Use these blends to make a word in each box. Draw a picture to illustrate your word.

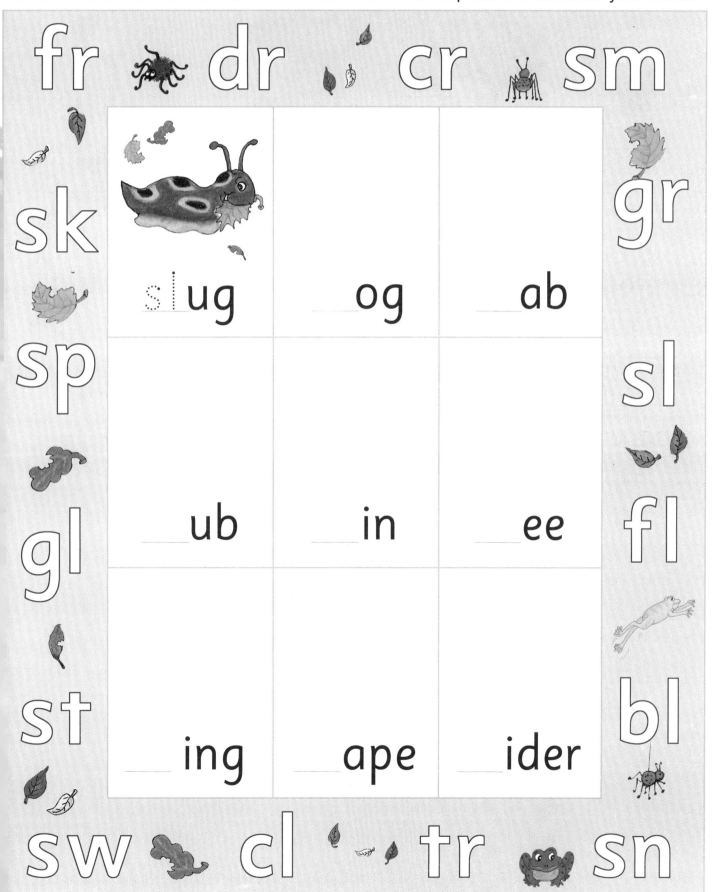

fr   dr   cr   sm

sk

sp

gl

st

gr

sl

fl

bl

s|ug   ___og   ___ab

___ub   ___in   ___ee

___ing   ___ape   ___ider

sw   cl   tr   sn

23

y

Action
Put your hands on your head like donkey's ears and say *ee*.

bed
wet
prod
holly
party
story
happy
so
my
family

Write a word with ‹y› at the end in each holly leaf and draw a picture.

holly

Dictation

1.

2.

3.

4.

5.

6.

7.

8.

9.

24

Initial Consonant Blends

Write the word underneath each picture. All the words have initial consonant blends.

grin

Read the words in the leaves. If the word has a short vowel sound, color the leaf's edge yellow.

a e i
o u

sad
let
trip
blue
orange
gray
black
one
by
color

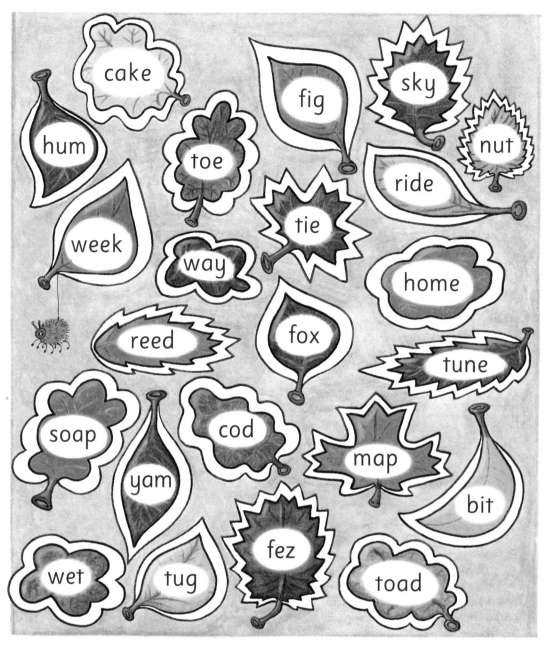

Dictation

1. _____

2. _____

3. _____

4. _____

5. _____

6. _____

7. _____

8. _____

9. _____

26

Alphabetical Order

When looking up words in a dictionary, it helps to think of the alphabet in sections. Trace inside each capital letter using a different color for each section of the alphabet. Write the lower-case letters next to the capital letters.

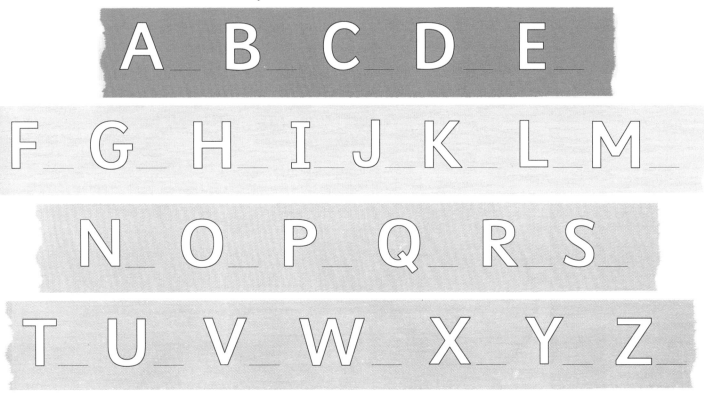

Dictionaries tell you how a word is spelled and what it means.
Find each letter in the dictionary and write down the first word beginning with that letter.

Aa _____	Gg _____
Nn _____	Oo _____
Ss _____	Zz _____

Put these sets of letters into alphabetical order.

a_e

Add ‹a_e› to make a word in each grape. Read and illustrate each word.

Action
Cup your hand over your ear and say *ai, ai, ai.*

ran
hat
scar
came
grape
name
cake
only
old
baseball

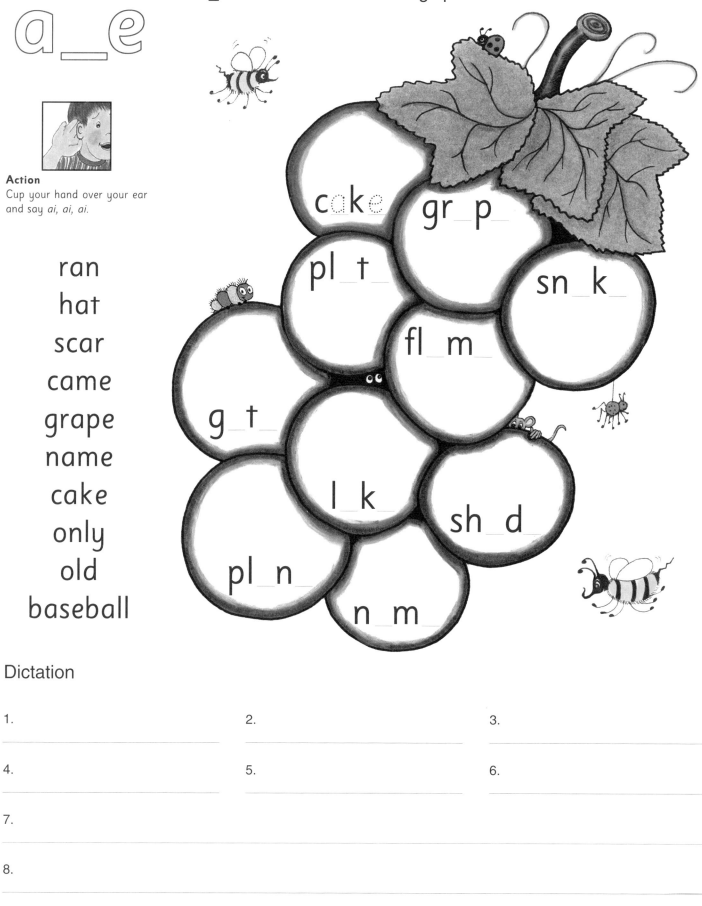

cake   gr_p_   pl_t_   sn_k_   fl_m_   g_t_   l_k   sh_d   pl_n_   n_m_

Dictation

1.

2.

3.

4.

5.

6.

7.

8.

9.

28

Verbs

Action
Move your arms back and forth at your sides, as if you are running.

Write the verb underneath each picture.

to _____   to _____   to _____

Draw a bee doing each verb.

to cry   to hop   to brush

Think of three more verbs and illustrate them in the flowers.

to _____   to _____   to _____

29

i_e

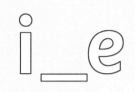

Action
Stand to attention and salute,
saying *ie, ie.*

six
pad
smell
bike
time
smile
prize
like
have
bridesmaid

Add ‹i_e› to make a word in each kite. Read and illustrate each word.

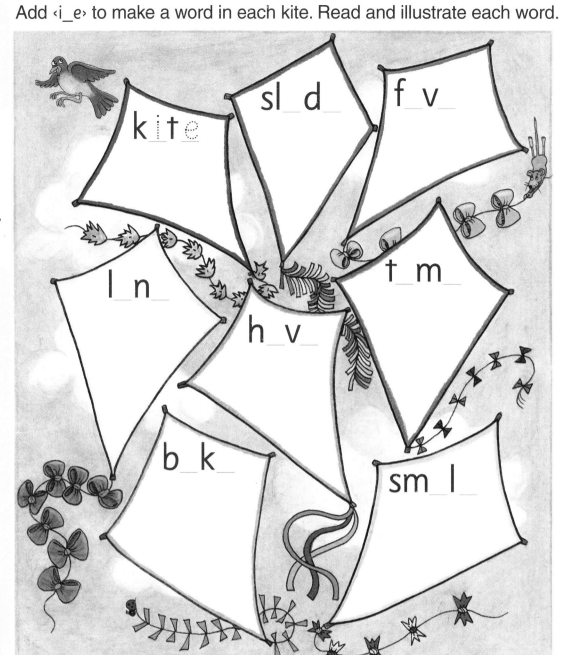

k i t e

sl_d_

f_v_

l_n_

h_v_

t_m_

b_k_

sm_l_

Dictation

1.

2.

3.

4.

5.

6.

7.

8.

9.

Verbs

Think of a verb and write it on the line.

to _____

Write the verb next to each pronoun, and draw a picture for each person doing the verb. Remember that the verb has an ‹s› at the end when joined to the third person singular, and that you must draw more than one person for the plural pronouns.

1st person singular	2nd person singular	3rd person singular

I _____   you _____

he
she _____
it

1st person plural	2nd person plural	3rd person plural

we _____   you _____   they _____

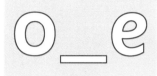

Action
Bring your hand over your mouth and say *oh!*

cod
lot
snap
bone
nose
home
globe
live
give
tadpole

Add ‹o_e› to make a word in each tadpole. Illustrate each word.

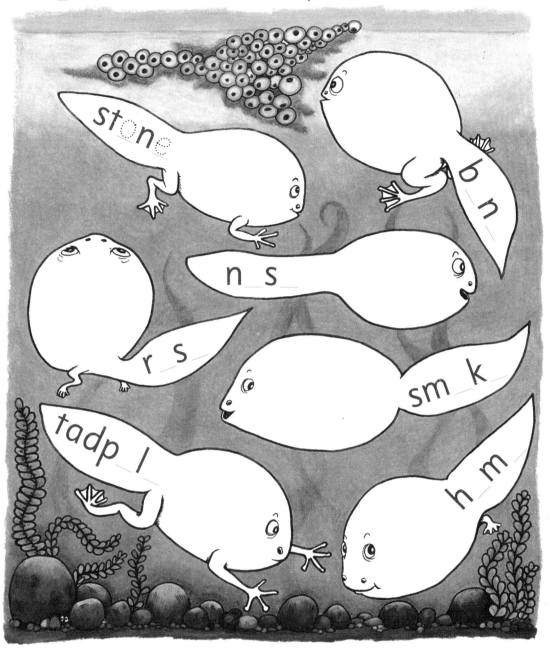

Dictation

1. _____   2. _____   3. _____

4. _____   5. _____   6. _____

7. _____

8. _____

9. _____

Verbs
past tense

Present Tense Action		Past Tense Action	
Point towards the floor with the palm of your hand.		Point backwards over your shoulder with your thumb.	

The simplest way to make the past tense is by adding ‹ed› to the verb.

Today, I **talk**. talk + ed Yesterday, I **talked**.

If a verb already ends with an ‹e›, cross it off before adding ‹ed›.

Today, I **smile**. smil~~e~~ + ed Yesterday, I **smiled**.

Put these verbs into the past tense.

Present	Past	Present	Past
jump	_____	hope	_____
paint	_____	play	_____
like	_____	wave	_____
shout	_____	skate	_____
rest	_____	twist	_____

Underline the verbs in red.
Then decide whether the sentences are in the present or the past.

She brushed her hair.   (past) / present

They look out of the window.   past / present

I cooked dinner.   past / present

The race started in the park.   past / present

33

Action
Point at people around you and say *you, you, you.*

bus
pot
swim
cube
tune
used
excuse
little
down
useless

Add ‹u_e› to make a word in each musical note. Illustrate each word.

Dictation

1.

2.

3.

4.

5.

6.

7.

8.

9.

34

Verbs

Write these verbs in the simple past tense.

bat

hop

pat

rip

nod

peg

hug

wag

hum

Write a ‹wh› word in each whale and draw a picture to illustrate it.

Action
Blow onto your open hands and say *wh, wh, wh.*

did
cut
twin
whale
wheel
white
whisper
what
when
whenever

Dictation

1. _____

2. _____

3. _____

4. _____

5. _____

6. _____

7. _____

8. _____

9. _____

36

Verbs
the future

Action
Point to the front.

Read the verbs in the *today* column. Then write the verbs in the past tense in the *yesterday* column, and in the future in the *tomorrow* column.

Past yesterday	Present today	Future tomorrow
I talked	I talk	I shall talk
I _____	I cook	I _____
I _____	I listen	I _____
I _____	I skate	I _____
I _____	I walk	I _____

Write some sentences about what you did yesterday.

_____

_____

_____

Write some sentences about what you will do tomorrow.

_____

_____

_____

ay

Action
Cup your hand over your ear
and say *ai, ai, ai.*

an
cat
skin
say
away
play
today
why
where
playground

Write an ‹ay› word in each crayon and draw a picture to illustrate it.

crayon

Dictation

1.

2.

3.

4.

5.

6.

7.

8.

9.

38

Alphabetical Order

a b c   d e   v w x y z

Write the capital letters next to the lower-case letters.

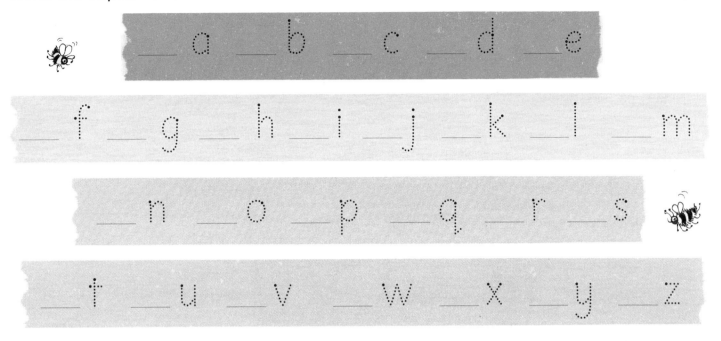

__ a __ b __ c __ d __ e

__ f __ g __ h __ i __ j __ k __ l __ m

__ n __ o __ p __ q __ r __ s

__ t __ u __ v __ w __ x __ y __ z

Put these sets of letters into alphabetical order.

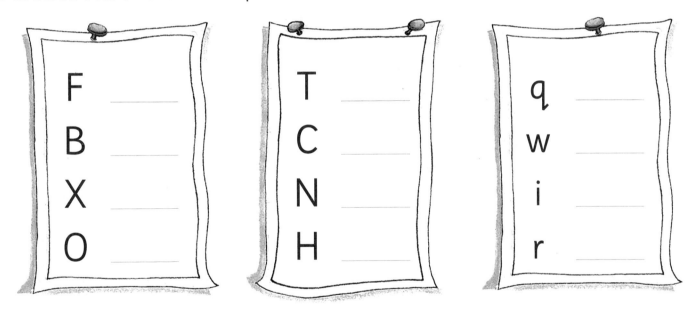

F _____
B _____
X _____
O _____

T _____
C _____
N _____
H _____

q _____
w _____
i _____
r _____

Put these sets of words into alphabetical order.

Inky _____
Snake _____
Bee _____

pear _____
apple _____
orange _____

39

ea

Action
Put your hands on your head like donkey's ears and say *ee*.

met
web
spin
tea
heat
leaf
each
who
which
seashell

Write an ‹ea› word in each teapot and draw a picture to illustrate it.

Dictation

1.

2.

3.

4.

5.

6.

7.

8.

9.

40

Nouns

Write six nouns for the things you can see in the picture.

a _____   the _____

a _____   the _____

a _____   the _____

Underline the nouns in black. There can be more than one noun in a sentence.

1. The cow is black and white.

2. Jim drives a red and yellow tractor.

3. The sheep graze on the hills.

4. On Andrew's farm, there are cows, sheep, chickens, and a horse.

igh

Action
Stand to attention and salute, saying *ie, ie*.

lip
his
went
night
high
might
light
any
many
frightening

Write an ‹igh› word in each light bulb and draw a picture.

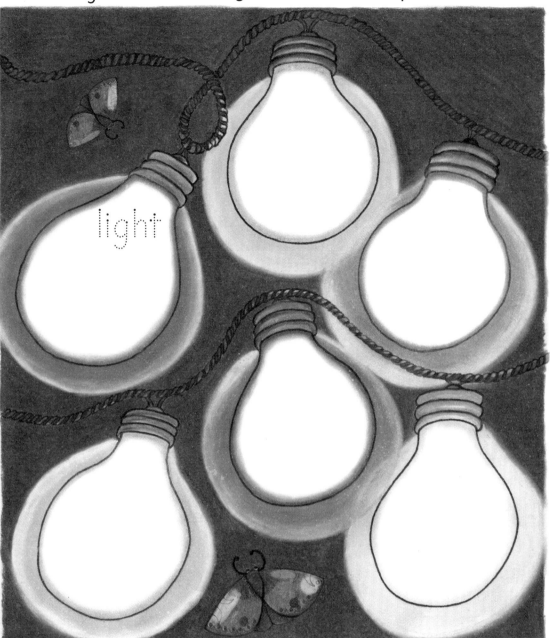

Dictation

1.

2.

3.

4.

5.

6.

7.

8.

9.

42

Adjectives

Action
Touch the side of your temple with your fist.

Color the snakes so that they match the adjectives.

You can use more than one adjective at a time. Color the snake to match your description.

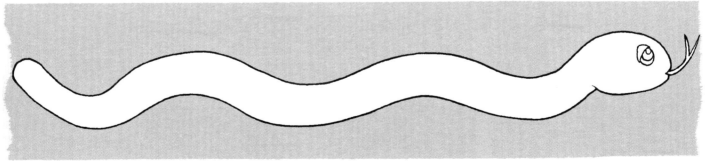

a _____, _____, _____ snake

43

y

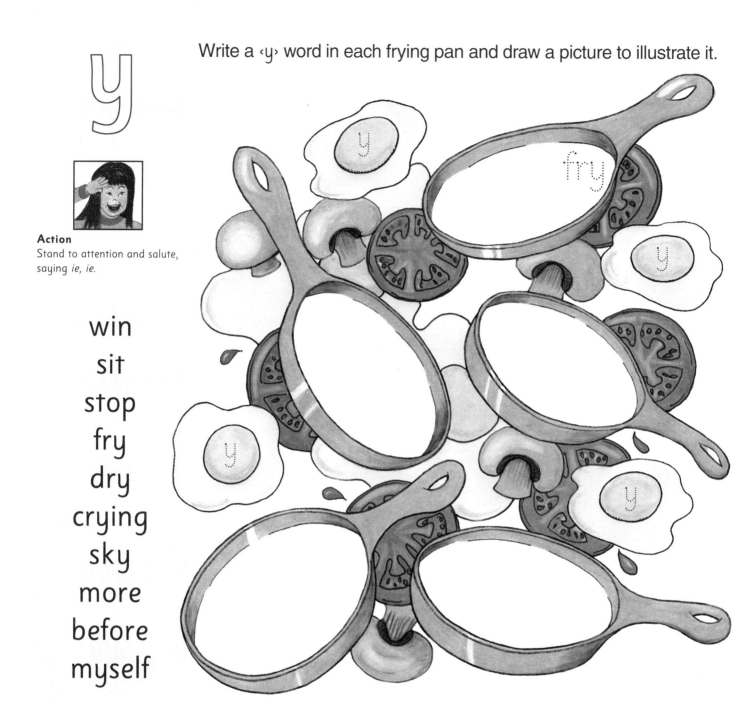

win
sit
stop
fry
dry
crying
sky
more
before
myself

Write a ‹y› word in each frying pan and draw a picture to illustrate it.

Dictation

1.

2.

3.

4.

5.

6.

7.

8.

9.

Adjectives

Underline the nouns in black. Find an adjective to describe each noun.
There are some adjectives in the snake to help you.

A _____ snake hisses.

My _____ shirt is new.

The _____ dog barks.

Her _____ car stopped.

The sky is _____ .

The tree is _____ .

The _____ flowers smell.

The show was _____ .

His _____ balloon burst.

My coat is _____ and _____ .

spotty

small

pink

tall

red

striped

green

long

yellow

floral

blue

Write an ‹ow› word in each snowman and draw a picture to illustrate it.

box
job
bulb
own
grow
elbow
yellow
other
were
snowman

snow

Dictation

1.

2.

3.

4.

5.

6.

7.

8.

9.

Final Consonant Blends

Read the final consonant blends at the top of the page and trace inside them. Use these blends to make a word in each box. Draw a picture to illustrate your word.

mp st lt nd nt sp

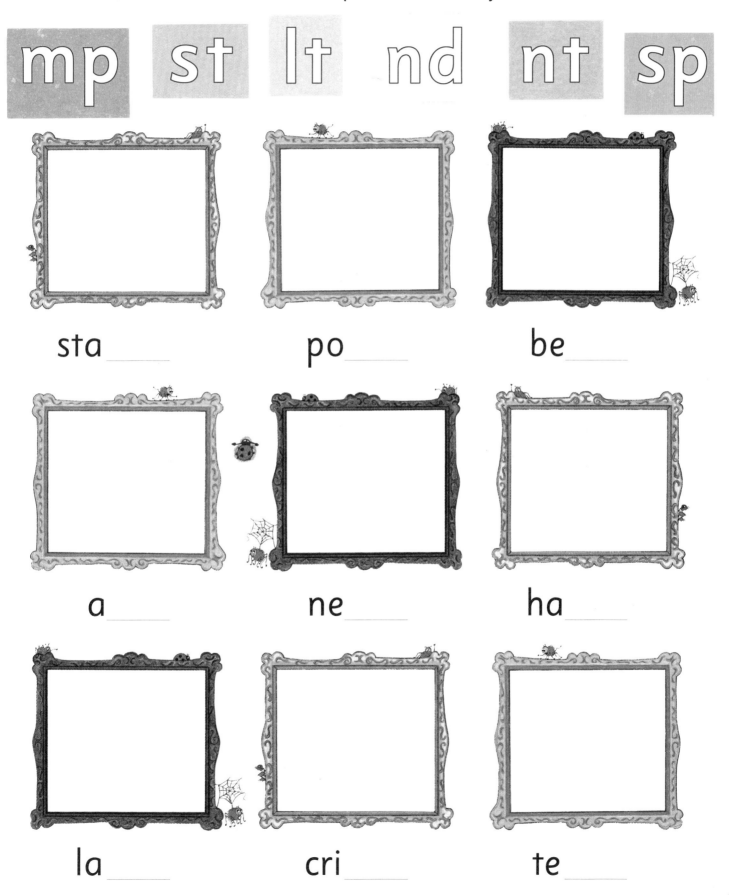

sta_____

po_____

be_____

a_____

ne_____

ha_____

la_____

cri_____

te_____

ew

Action
Point at people around you and say *you, you, you.*

Action
Move your head forward and say *oo.*

bud
sun
held
few
flew
grew
chew
because
want
newspaper

Write an ‹ew› word in each jewel and draw a picture to illustrate it.

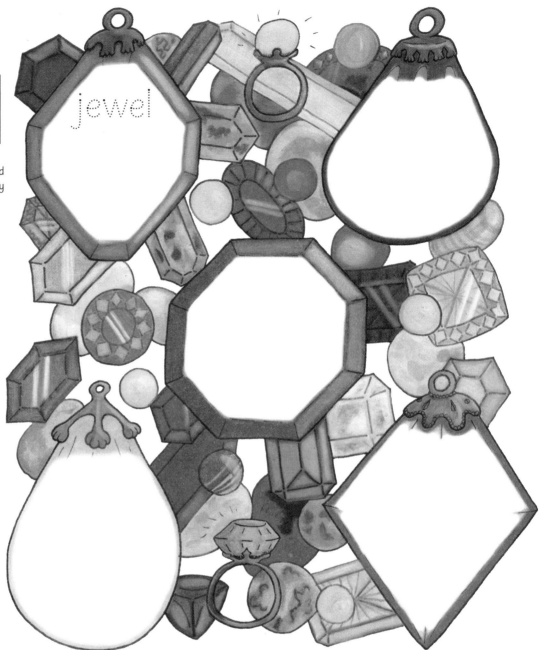

Dictation

1.

2.

3.

4.

5.

6.

7.

8.

9.

Compound Words

The compound word birds have muddled up their tails. Can you sort them out?
Color the tails to match the bodies.

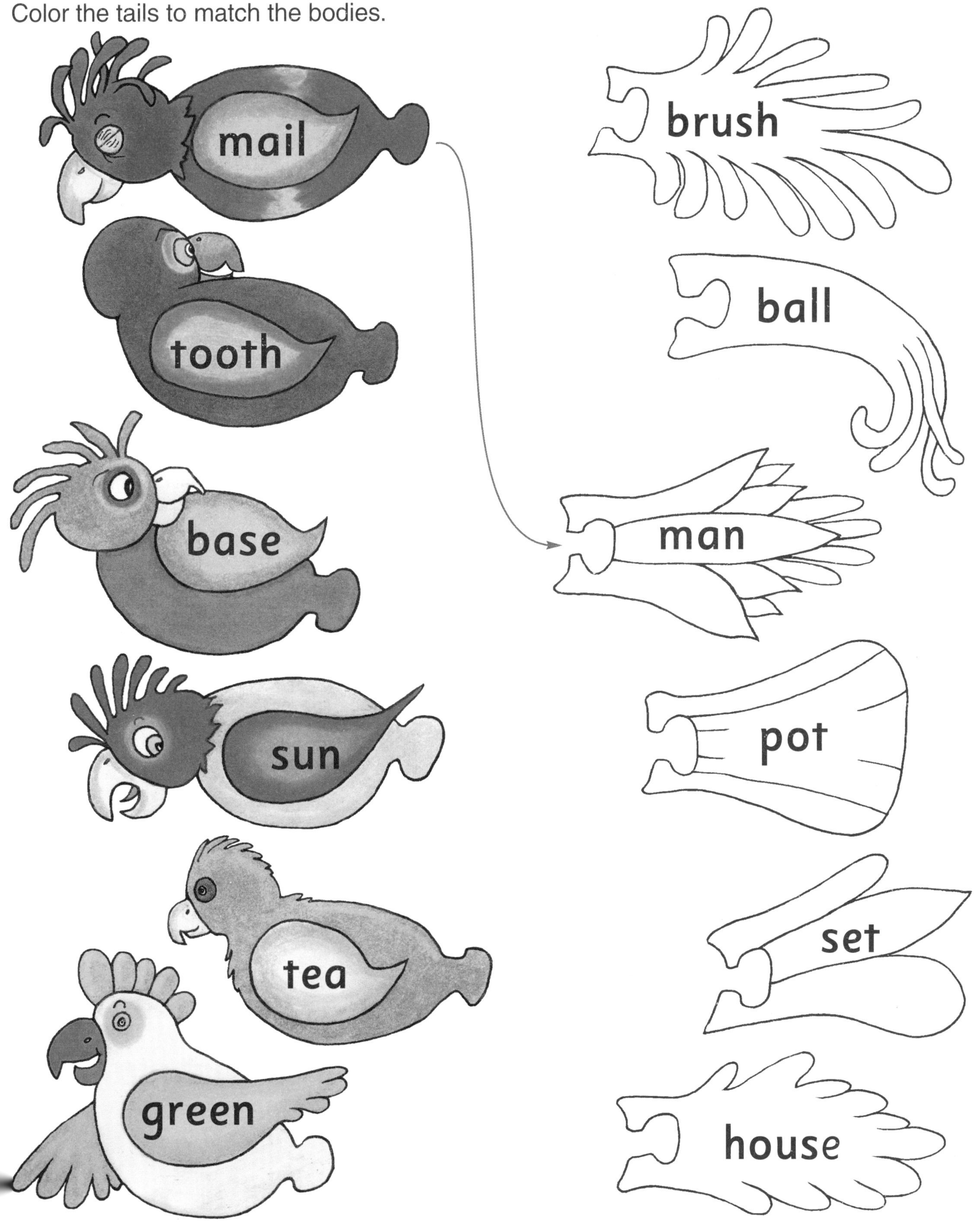

mail

tooth

base

sun

tea

green

brush

ball

man

pot

set

house

Action
Pretend your finger is a needle and prick your thumb, saying *ou, ou, ou.*

bat

pet

self

out

our

round

mouth

saw

put

outside

Write an ‹ou› word in each house and draw a picture to illustrate it.

Dictation

1.

2.

3.

4.

5.

6.

7.

8.

9.

50

Alphabetical Order

Put these sets of words into alphabetical order.

1.   car   truck   bus

a._____ b._____ c._____

2.   hamster   cat   rabbit

a._____ b._____ c._____

3.   lemon   apple   banana

a._____ b._____ c._____

4.   Sam   Mark   Rasheed   Greg

a._____ b._____ c._____ d._____

5.   Emily   Sue   Donna   Jennifer   Jill

a._____ b._____ c._____ d._____ e._____

ABCDEFGHIJKLMNOPQRSTUVWXYZ

Look up the words for these nouns in your dictionary. Carefully copy out the words.

_____   _____   _____

51

OW

big
fox
milk
how
owl
brown
town
could
should
flowerpot

Write an ‹ow› word in each owl and draw a picture to illustrate it.

owl

Dictation

1.

2.

3.

4.

5.

6.

7.

8.

9.

52

Verbs

Write six verbs for the actions you can see in the picture.

to _____   to _____

to _____   to _____

to _____   to _____

Underline the verbs in red. There can be more than one verb in a sentence.

1. Hannah smiled at her friend.

2. Carlos sails a boat.

3. Todd swims and dives in the sea.

4. The boys make a sand castle and then play ball.

53

oi

Action
Cup your hands around your mouth and shout *oi, ship ahoy!*

bug
had
film
oi
coin
noisy
toil
would
right
boiling

Write an ‹oi› word in each oil can and draw a picture to illustrate it.

Dictation

1. _____

2. _____

3. _____

4. _____

5. _____

6. _____

7. _____

8. _____

9. _____

Adverbs

Action
Bang one fist on top of the other.

Choose an adverb to go with each picture.

quickly   hungrily   slowly

secretly   happily   loudly

Inky eats

Snake slithers

Bee buzzes

The ants whisper

The snail goes

The band played

oy

jet
dig
help
boy
toy
enjoy
annoy
two
four
destroy

Write an ‹oy› word in each toy and draw a picture to illustrate it.

toys

Dictation

1.

2.

3.

4.

5.

6.

7.

8.

9.

Adverbs

Read the adverbs below, then read the story in the beehive.
Write an adverb in each space.

Bee's Busy Day

Bee woke up _____,
and traipsed _____ down
the hive to have breakfast.
She buzzed _____ as she
flew to the farm. She _____
collected as much pollen as she
could, and flew _____ back to
the hive. She smiled _____ to
herself. Bee, and her friends Inky
and Snake, had planned a day out.

or

Action
Put your hands on your head pointing down, like donkey's ears, and say *or*.

got
bun
belt
fork
storm
horse
forty
goes
does
morning

Write an ‹or› word in each horse and draw a picture to illustrate it.

horse

Dictation

1.

2.

3.

4.

5.

6.

7.

8.

9.

58

Plurals ‹es›

In the first column, write a noun ending in ‹sh›, ‹ch›, ‹s›, or ‹x› and draw a picture.
Write the plural of each noun in the second column.

sh

brush   brushes

ch

s

x

59

al

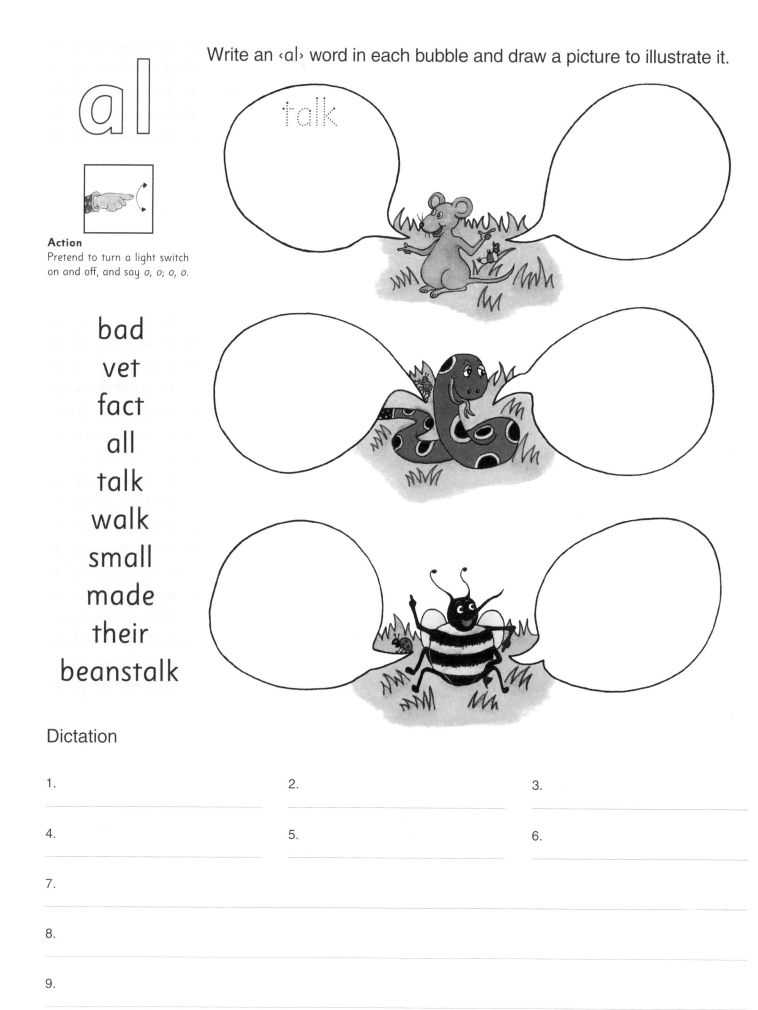

Action
Pretend to turn a light switch on and off, and say *o, o; o, o.*

Write an ‹al› word in each bubble and draw a picture to illustrate it.

talk

bad
vet
fact
all
talk
walk
small
made
their
beanstalk

Dictation

1.

2.

3.

4.

5.

6.

7.

8.

9.

60

Opposites

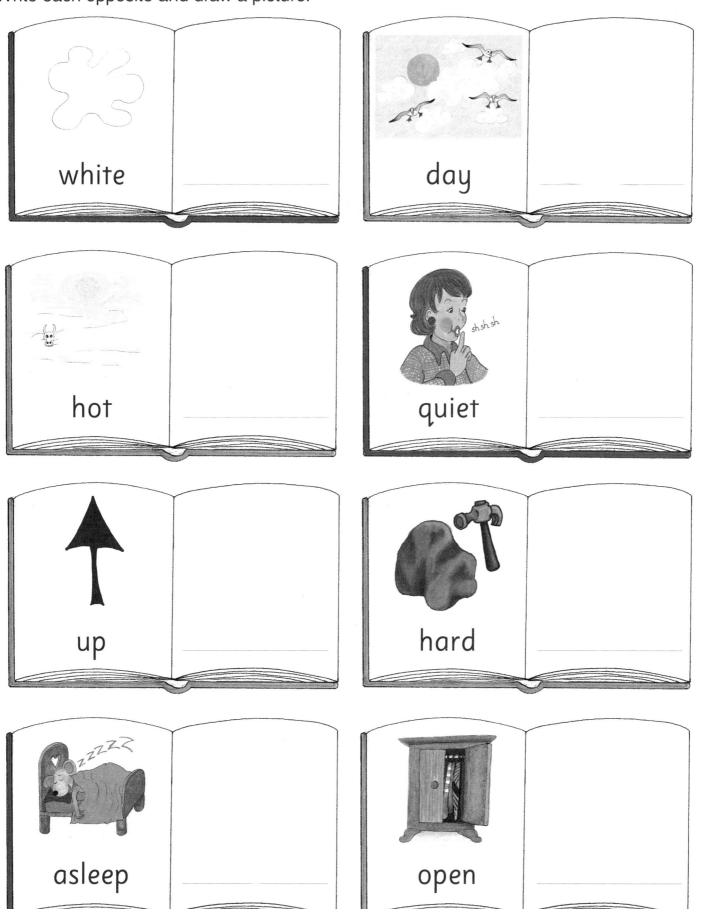

Antonyms

Write each opposite and draw a picture.

white

day

hot

quiet

up

hard

asleep

open

61

nk

Action
Pretend to lift a heavy weight above your head and say *ng*.

Action
Snap your fingers together, saying *ck, ck, ck.*

fin
sob
left
sink
pink
drink
think
once
upon
winking

Write an ‹nk› word in each drink and draw a picture to illustrate it.

drink

Dictation

1.

2.

3.

4.

5.

6.

7.

8.

9.

Using a Dictionary

We can use a dictionary to check how to spell words.
Look up each word in your dictionary to circle the right spelling.

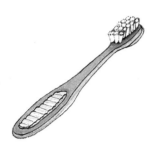

toofbrush
toothbrush

rabbit
rabit

starr
star

octopus
octapus

flouer
flower

buterfie
butterfly

These words are spelled incorrectly. Look them up and copy out the correct spelling.

boock   **carpit**   **triangel**

_____   _____   _____

We can also use a dictionary to find out what a word means.
Look up these words and write down their meanings.

atlas _____

_____

yacht _____

_____

er

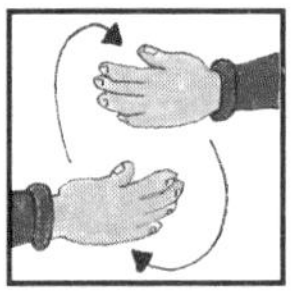

Action
Action
Roll your hands over each other like a mixer, saying *erererererer*.

Write an ‹er› word in each gingerbread man and draw a picture.

term

er

er

mud
jam
sent
term
summer
river
number
always
also
woodpecker

Dictation

1.

2.

3.

4.

5.

6.

7.

8.

9.

64

"Speech Marks"

What are these animals saying?
Write their speech inside the speech bubbles, and then in between speech marks.

said the bee.   said the snake.   said the bird.

said the cow.   said the donkey.   said the duck.

ir

Action
Roll your hands over each other like a mixer, saying *erererererer*.

yet
hid
wept
skirt
girl
shirt
first
of
eight
birthday

Write an ‹ir› word in each bird and draw a picture to illustrate it.

Dictation

1.

2.

3.

4.

5.

6.

7.

8.

9.

Word Web

How many words could you use instead of *said?* Write the words in the word web.

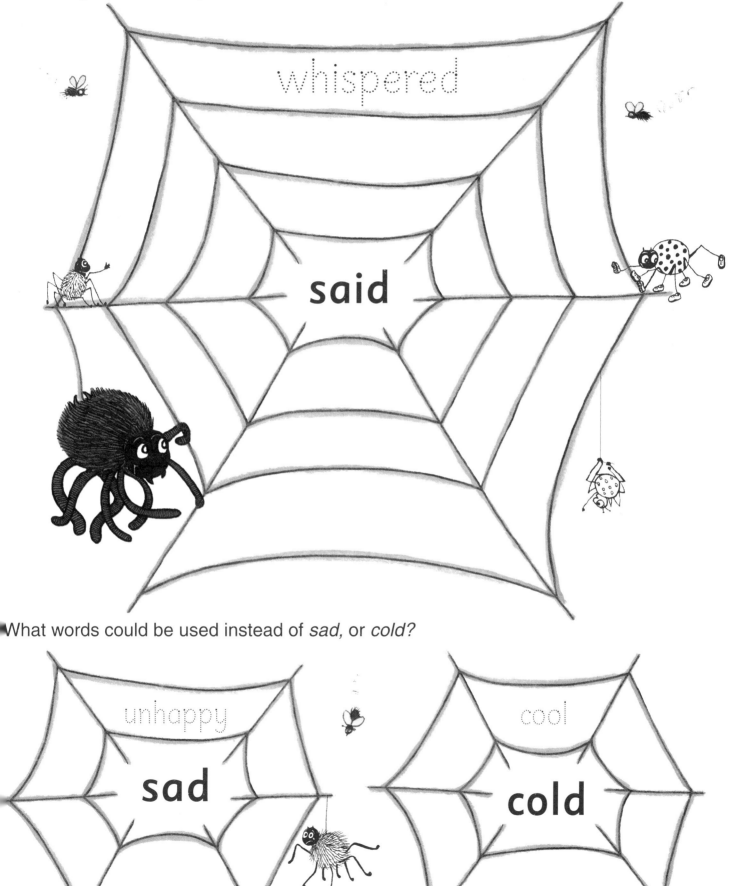

whispered

said

What words could be used instead of *sad,* or *cold?*

unhappy

sad

cool

cold

ur

Write a ‹ur› word in each turkey and draw a picture to illustrate it.

Action
Roll your hands over each other like a mixer, saying *erererererer*.

not
sum
next
turn
nurse
turkey
purple
love
cover
hamburger

turkey

Dictation

1. _____

2. _____

3. _____

4. _____

5. _____

6. _____

7. _____

8. _____

9. _____

Questions

We use these words to ask questions.

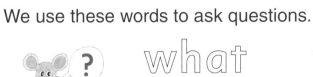 

what   why   when
where   who   which

Trace inside the question marks, using different colors.

Answer these questions.

1. What is your name? _____

2. Where do you live? _____

3. When is your birthday? _____

If you met someone for the first time, what questions would you ask them?

_____

_____

_____

_____

_____

au

Action
Pretend to turn a light switch on and off, and say *o, o; o, o.*

map
fix
jump
fault
pause
haunt
August
after
every
astronaut

Write an ‹au› word in each astronaut and draw a picture.

Dictation

Questions

You ask questions to find things out.

what   where   when   why   who   which

Choose a question word to fit each sentence.

1. _____ won the quiz?

2. _____ time is it?

3. _____ book do you like best?

4. _____ are you going this summer?

5. _____ did you do that?

6. _____ can we play basketball?

Read the questions and answers and see if you can guess which animal the girl is thinking of.

1. Do you have fur?
2. How many legs do you have?
3. Do you have long ears?
4. What do you eat?

Yes

Four

Yes

Carrots, oats, and grass

Which animal is it?

Find a partner and play the game yourself.

Write an ‹aw› word in each saw and draw a picture to illustrate it.

zip
men
pond
saw
claw
dawn
prawn
mother
father
strawberry

Dictation

1. _____

2. _____

3. _____

4. _____

5. _____

6. _____

7. _____

8. _____

9. _____

Read the story below. Then underline the nouns in black and the verbs in red.

Nouns

Verbs

Inky toils long and hard in the garden. She digs the brown earth. The birds watch her interestedly. They wait eagerly for the grubs.

In the spring, Inky plants the seeds in the ground. She grows orange carrots, crispy lettuces, and tall, green beans. In summer, she carefully harvests the yummy vegetables and eats them.

Inky also grows tall, yellow sunflowers in the garden. She likes the lovely sunflowers. The birds also like the sunflowers. They hungrily eat the striped black and white seeds.

Now see if you can underline the pronouns in pink, the adjectives in blue, and the adverbs in orange.

Pronouns

Adjectives

Adverbs

73

Spellings

Spelling Test 1	Spelling Test 2	Spelling Test 3
1.	1.	1.
2.	2.	2.
3.	3.	3.
4.	4.	4.
5.	5.	5.
6.	6.	6.
7.	7.	7.
8.	8.	8.
9.	9.	9.
10.	10.	10.

Spelling Test 4	Spelling Test 5	Spelling Test 6
1.	1.	1.
2.	2.	2.
3.	3.	3.
4.	4.	4.
5.	5.	5.
6.	6.	6.
7.	7.	7.
8.	8.	8.
9.	9.	9.
10.	10.	10.

Spellings

Spelling Test 7

1. _____
2. _____
3. _____
4. _____
5. _____
6. _____
7. _____
8. _____
9. _____
10. _____

Spelling Test 8

1. _____
2. _____
3. _____
4. _____
5. _____
6. _____
7. _____
8. _____
9. _____
10. _____

Spelling Test 9

1. _____
2. _____
3. _____
4. _____
5. _____
6. _____
7. _____
8. _____
9. _____
10. _____

Spelling Test 10

1. _____
2. _____
3. _____
4. _____
5. _____
6. _____
7. _____
8. _____
9. _____
10. _____

Spelling Test 11

1. _____
2. _____
3. _____
4. _____
5. _____
6. _____
7. _____
8. _____
9. _____
10. _____

Spelling Test 12

1. _____
2. _____
3. _____
4. _____
5. _____
6. _____
7. _____
8. _____
9. _____
10. _____

Spellings

Spelling Test 13	Spelling Test 14	Spelling Test 15
1.	1.	1.
2.	2.	2.
3.	3.	3.
4.	4.	4.
5.	5.	5.
6.	6.	6.
7.	7.	7.
8.	8.	8.
9.	9.	9.
10.	10.	10.

Spelling Test 16	Spelling Test 17	Spelling Test 18
1.	1.	1.
2.	2.	2.
3.	3.	3.
4.	4.	4.
5.	5.	5.
6.	6.	6.
7.	7.	7.
8.	8.	8.
9.	9.	9.
10.	10.	10.

Spellings

Spelling Test 19

1. _____
2. _____
3. _____
4. _____
5. _____
6. _____
7. _____
8. _____
9. _____
10. _____

Spelling Test 20

1. _____
2. _____
3. _____
4. _____
5. _____
6. _____
7. _____
8. _____
9. _____
10. _____

Spelling Test 21

1. _____
2. _____
3. _____
4. _____
5. _____
6. _____
7. _____
8. _____
9. _____
10. _____

Spelling Test 22

1. _____
2. _____
3. _____
4. _____
5. _____
6. _____
7. _____
8. _____
9. _____
10. _____

Spelling Test 23

1. _____
2. _____
3. _____
4. _____
5. _____
6. _____
7. _____
8. _____
9. _____
10. _____

Spelling Test 24

1. _____
2. _____
3. _____
4. _____
5. _____
6. _____
7. _____
8. _____
9. _____
10. _____

Spellings

Spelling Test 25	Spelling Test 26	Spelling Test 27
1.	1.	1.
2.	2.	2.
3.	3.	3.
4.	4.	4.
5.	5.	5.
6.	6.	6.
7.	7.	7.
8.	8.	8.
9.	9.	9.
10.	10.	10.

Spelling Test 28	Spelling Test 29	Spelling Test 30
1.	1.	1.
2.	2.	2.
3.	3.	3.
4.	4.	4.
5.	5.	5.
6.	6.	6.
7.	7.	7.
8.	8.	8.
9.	9.	9.
10.	10.	10.

Spellings

Spelling Test 31

1. _____
2. _____
3. _____
4. _____
5. _____
6. _____
7. _____
8. _____
9. _____
10. _____

Spelling Test 32

1. _____
2. _____
3. _____
4. _____
5. _____
6. _____
7. _____
8. _____
9. _____
10. _____

Spelling Test 33

1. _____
2. _____
3. _____
4. _____
5. _____
6. _____
7. _____
8. _____
9. _____
10. _____

Spelling Test 34

1. _____
2. _____
3. _____
4. _____
5. _____
6. _____
7. _____
8. _____
9. _____
10. _____

Spelling Test 35

1. _____
2. _____
3. _____
4. _____
5. _____
6. _____
7. _____
8. _____
9. _____
10. _____

Spelling Test 36

1. _____
2. _____
3. _____
4. _____
5. _____
6. _____
7. _____
8. _____
9. _____
10. _____